Hello

Welcome to Dive D⌐

The story was serialised on Facebook,
Instagram, Google+ and Tumblr, and the first
100 printed copies given away, with some
hidden in different locations.
The purchase of this print on demand version
supports the project and our aim to help the
seals to swim far and wide, connecting with the
people who need them. Thank you.

You can find out more at
DiveDownTheBook.com

I'd love to hear from you:

info@samdrawsthings.co.uk
@samdrawsthings
on Twitter and Instagram
SamDrawsThingsIllustration on Facebook
sam-draws-things.tumblr.com
google.com/+SamanthaGoodlet

You can also find a Dive Down
Spotify playlist to accompany the story here:

For everyone that was a part of
my safety net

Thank you.

At the time of printing, all links and
references in the back of the book
were correct.

Please visit
www.DiveDownTheBook.com
for more information, free digital
versions of the story and further links.

Dive Down:

Drawings from the deep

A story about
discovering beauty

Illustrations by Sam Draws Things
Words by Sam Attenborough

One foot in front of the other...

I just keep walking.

Where am I going?

Maybe I could stop.

And let go...

...am I falling or flying?

falling

Ah! There's a safety net.

I'll rest here for a while.

That was lovely,

but it's time to go.

Here I go...

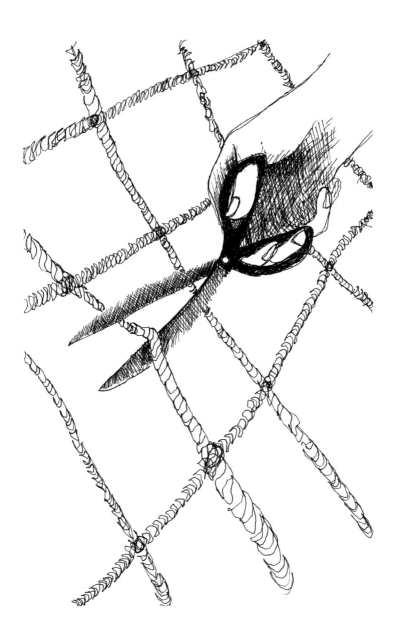

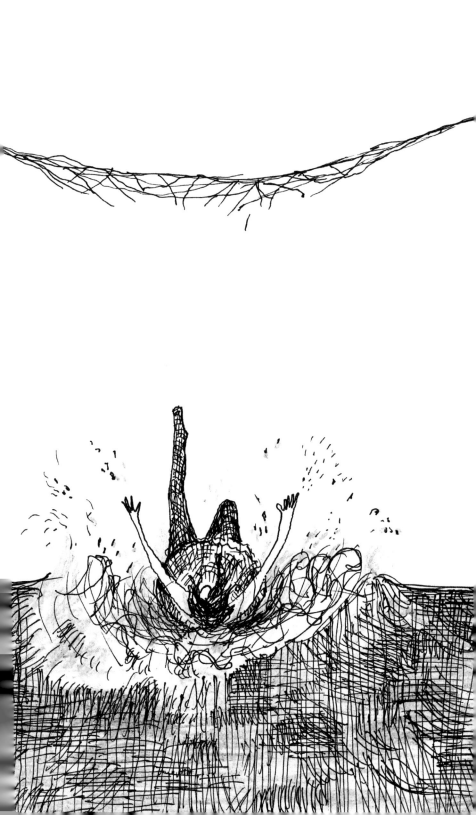

Immersion.

Breathing in.

Breathing out.

Let's go deeper...

And deeper...

And deeper...

Deeper still...

I'm still safe.

I start to notice.

And feel freer.

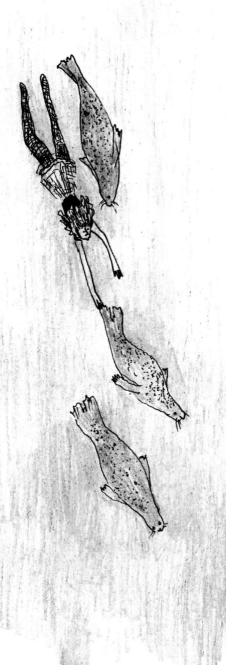

It's beautiful,

I didn't realise.

Beauty is everywhere,

everywhere.

Further down.

It's beautiful here too.

Even here.

Moving and flowing.

I'm playing.

It feels solid,

I am safe.

I know who I am.

Let's dance!

And share.

Be with life

and love.

I feel alive.

I love life.

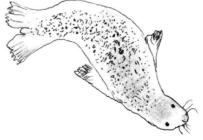

Further reading

These illustrations were created during a quiet time of reflection. I didn't know where the story was going - I was just diving in, drawing as I read, thought and realised.

Here are some useful resources for other deep sea divers...

Self help & healing

When things fall apart: Heart advice for difficult times
by Pema Chödrön
A book of advice and meditations based on Buddhist principles. Not just for tough times, it helps redefine hope and happiness and at any point in your life.
pemachodron foundation.org

The Ram Dass Love Serve Remember Foundation
A website, app and Facebook page sharing daily words of wisdom, lectures and meditations from the amazing Ram Dass.
ramdass.org

Women Who Run with the Wolves: Myths and Stories of the Wild Woman Archetype
by Clarissa Pinkola Estes
A beautiful book that analyses fairy stories and folk tales to help women reconnect with their wild, creative, inner selves.
clarissapinkolaestes. com

Mind
A UK-based charity offering support for anyone stuggling with mental health issues
mind.org.uk

Find a Counsellor
A UK based website helping match you to therapists and counsellors in your area
findacounsellor.info

To Write Love on Her Arms
A US based charity offering support and inspiration for people struggling with addiction, depression, self-injury and thoughts of suicide
twloha.com

Chasers of the Light: Poems from the Typewriter Series
by Tyler Knott Gregson
Uplifting poetry and photos inspired by love and life
tylerknott.com

5 Rhythms Dance
A therapeutic approach to dance as a moving form of meditation, founded by Gabrielle Roth
5rhythms.com

Seals & Selkies

There are two main species of Seals found in UK waters - the Harbour or Common Seal (Phoca vitulina) and the Grey Seal (Halichoerus grypus). You can find out more about their status and conservation here:
chartingprogress.defra. gov.uk/seals

Blakeney Point in Norfolk is an amazing spot where you can take boat trips to see both seal species in their natural habitat.
nationaltrust.org.uk/ blakeney

The Selkies or Seal People are found in Celtic mythology. They can switch between human and seal form - often beautiful humans with large brown eyes, sometimes taking revenge on people who hurt seals. You can read more in
Land of the Seal People by Duncan Williamson.

There's more at
DiveDownTheBook.com

12128501R00039

Printed in Great Britain
by Amazon.co.uk, Ltd.,
Marston Gate.